Sacred Numerology

With Sue Frederick, author of I See Your Dream Job; I See Your Soul Mate; Bridges to Heaven; Your Divine Lens & Water Oak

www.SueFrederick.com

Sue@Brilliantwork.com

Copyright © 2023 by Sue Frederick
All rights reserved.
ISBN: 978-0-9762393-6-9

Author's Bio

- **Sue Frederick** is an ordained Unity Minister, master numerologist, lifelong intuitive, Past Life & Between Lives Soul Regression Therapist.

- She's the author of: **Through a Divine Lens; Practices to quiet your ego & align with your soul; Bridges to Heaven: True Stories of Loved Ones on the Other Side; I See Your Soul Mate & I See Your Dream Job (St. Martin's Press)**.

- As an intuitive coach, she's helped thousands of people realign with their soul's purpose and connect to departed loved ones for healing conversations.

- Her work has been featured in the New York Times, CNN.com, Real Simple, Yoga Journal, Natural Health and Complete Woman Magazines.

- Her popular **Mystical Conversations Podcast** is available on Apple Podcasts and other venues.

- http://www.SueFrederick.com

Table of Contents

History & Meaning of Numbers – Page 1

Reduce to a Single Digit – Page 3

Calculate Your Birth Path – Page 5

Master Numbers 11, 22, 33 – Page 7

Linear, Stacked & Single Digit Methods – Page 9

3 Ways to Add Birth Dates – Page 11

Positive & Negative Meaning of Numbers – Page 13

Astrology Sun Signs – Page 19

Soul Agreements – Page 29

Name Number – Page 41

Pinnacle Cycles – Page 47

Personal Year Cycles – Page 51

Saturn Returns – Page 59

Birth Path Charts – Page 63

www.SueFrederick.com

History & Meaning of Numbers

- Greek philosopher and mystic Pythagoras, father of our modern number system, designed a theory of numbers based on the digits 1 through 9 in 580 BC.

- Pythagoras taught that each number has a meaning or vibration and by adding the numbers within your birth date and reducing them to single digits, you reveal the nature of the work you came here to do.

- Today we still use the number system Pythagoras created but we've disregarded the core meaning that was central to his system -that each number carries a meaning that goes beyond mere quantity.

Positive & Negative Energy of Numbers

- In Pythagoras' system every number has a positive and negative vibration which shows its potentials and challenges. Your destiny number, which is derived from your birth date contains the vibrations of the greatness you came to achieve along with the potential pitfalls of your path.

- All numbers are reduced to digits 1 through 9 except for three cosmic vibrations symbolized by the master numbers 11, 22 & 33.

Reduce to Single Digits

- All other numbers are reduced to the basic digits 1 through 9 by adding the digits of the entire number together.

- For example: the number 43 equals 7
- (4 + 3 = 7)

- The number 10 equals 1
- (1 + 0 = 1)

Birth Path is your Soul's Mission

- **Example of Birth Path Calculation:**
- Birth Date: **October 16, 1980**

- Month = October = 10 = 1 (1+0 = 1)
- Date = 16 = 7 (1+6 = 7)
- Year = 1980 = 9
  (1+9+8+0 = 18) (1+8 = 9)

- Birth Path = 8 (1+7+9 = 17 = 8)

Calculate your birth path:

To calculate **your birth path** from your date of birth:

Your birth month: Feb = 2

Your birth date: 17 = 8

Your birth year: 1952 = 8

Total: 2 + 8 + 8 = 18 = 9

Reduced to a single digit: 9

Your birth path number: 9

Master Numbers 11, 22, 33

The **Master Soul Numbers** of 11, 22 & 33 represent sacred birth paths designed to help humanity evolve. Those numbers are not reduced to a single digit in birth path calculations.
Example:

Birth Date **Sept 15, 1951**

September = 9
15 = 6 (1 + 5 = 6)
1951 = 7 (1+9+5+1=16) (1+6=7)

Total 22 master path soul (9+6+7=22)

Linear, Stacked & Single Digit Methods

- It's important to add each birth date **three different ways** to check your addition & to look for hidden master path numbers.

- This is especially important if you've arrived at a 2, 4, or 6 birth path which could contain a hidden 11, 22, or 33 path if added two other ways.

- **The three ways are:**
- **The Linear method:**
- **The Stacked Method:**
- **The Single Digit Method**

3 Ways to Add Birth Dates

- Using Birth Date **May 1, 1960**

- **Linear Method**: 5+1+1+9+6+0 = 22/4 Path

- **Stacked Method**:   **Single Digit Method:**

	Stacked			Single Digit
	5	=		5
	1	=		1
+	1960	=	16 =	+7
	1966 = 22/4 Path			13/4 Path

Positive & Negative meaning of numbers

- 1 - Leadership, vision, independence **OR** Loneliness, self-doubt, arrogance

- 2 - Intuition, understanding, detail **OR** dependency, paranoia, obsession with meaningless details

- 3 - Self expressive, creative, uplifting **OR** coldhearted, overintellectual, lack of responsibility

- 4 - Self discipline, strength, determination, practicality **OR** too practical, lost in drudgery & routine

- 5 - Change, sensuality, freedom, passion **OR** over- indulgence, addictions, impulsive & uncentered

- 6 - Social consciousness, healer, teacher **OR** slave to others needs, supercritical of loved ones.

- 7 - Intellectual & spiritual focus, wise, dignified, refined **OR** isolated, hypersensitive, skeptical.

- 8 - Power, wealth, accomplishment & generosity **OR** abusive, manipulative & controlling.

- 9 - Humanitarian, accomplished, artistic **OR** bitter, blameful & focused on past.

More...

- 11 - Intuitive, artistic, humanitarian, healer **OR** too sensitive & egocentric.

- 22 - Inspired visionary, practical genius **OR** greedy, abusive & lost in drudgery.

- 33 – Visionary artist, clairvoyant, master healer OR hyper-sensitive, lost in addictions & disconnected from others.

To learn more...

- To apply the numbers specifically to birth paths see **Chapter 7** page 56 of Sue's book *I See Your Dream Job – available on Amazon*.

- **Sue's book *I See Your Soul Mate* also explains the numbers, birth paths, personal years and soul agreements very clearly.**

- **Sue's book *Bridges to Heaven* explains how the numbers and paths apply to healing grief and loss.**

www.SueFrederick.com

Astrology Sun Signs

- How do the numbers in the birth date interface with **Astrology**? In many ways.

- However we're keeping it simple here and focusing on how the sun sign interacts with and flavors the birth path.

Astrology Sun Signs

- Aries = Ram = March 21 - April 19
- Taurus = Bull = April 20 - May 20
- Gemini = Twins = May 21 - June 21
- Cancer = Crab = June 22 - July 22
- Leo = Lion = July 23 - August 22
- Virgo = Virgin = August 23 - Sept 22

Sun Signs

- Libra = Scales = Sept 23 - Oct 23
- Scorpio = Scorpion = Oct 24 - Nov 21
- Sagittarius = Archer = Nov 22 - Dec 21
- Capricorn = Goat = Dec 22 - Jan 19
- Aquarius = Water Bearer = Jan 20 - Feb 18
- Pisces = Fish = Feb 19 - March 20

Birth Path & Sun Sign work together....

- Your sun sign reveals the flavor of your work mission. Someone who is on a 7 path with an Aries sun sign will fulfill their destiny with a different style than someone on a 7 path with a Pisces sun sign.

- **By combining the birth path number & sun sign**, you will get more specific ideas about the person's true work.

- For examples, read **Chapter 9** page 74 of *I See Your Dream Job*.

- **Aries (Ram) = March 21 – April 19**
- If you wrapped your Birth Path number with Aries, you will be powerful and bold - leading others to new ideas.

- **Taurus (Bull) = April 20 – May 20**
- If Taurus is the flavor you chose, you're made of pure force and solid will-power. Being practical puts you at ease. You may take awhile to get going on your higher mission, and it's essential that you loosen your tight grip on practicality in order to fulfill your potential.

Sun Sign meanings...

- **Gemini (Twins) = May 21 – June 21**
- Your agile, hungry mind is a great gift, but it can distract you from the intuitive knowledge of what's right for your life. You'll change perspectives frequently and become quite brilliant, cunning, and accomplished. Let your heart and intuition serve as your compass, or you'll lose your way and fall far offpath.
- **Cancer (Crab) = June 22 – July 22**
- Your heightened sensitivity and secretive nature is your gift and challenge. You feel everything and process it through your silent filter - rather than readily sharing it with others. Yet your feelings and intuitions are your gift. Don't hide that brilliant wisdom and retreat into self doubt and fear. Show your sensitivity to the world, bare your sweet soul, and speak the truth.

Sun Sign meanings...

- **Leo (Lion) = July 23 – August 22**
- The majestic, warm, and kindly lion, Leo rules with generosity of spirit and fiery passion. Your noble and confident presence will dominate any environment you work in. But don't get lost in "showmanship." Reach deep into your essence for the purpose of this great path – lighting the fire of higher knowledge.
- **Virgo (Virgin) = August 23 – September 22**
- The ultimate seeker of truth and understanding, your relentless analysis and pursuit of perfection is your gift and curse. In any career, you'll get to the core of the problem and perceive the essential truth instantly. Your challenge is to refrain from pointing out those flaws and imperfections, until you've found solutions.

Sun Sign Meanings

- **Libra (Scales) = Sept 23 – Oct 23**
- Grace, beauty, truth, and fairness flavor your mission. Rather than focusing on injustices, you'll create solutions. Your abundant talents will find a home in the arts - whether you choose acting, dance, writing, or design.

- **Scorpio (Scorpion) = Oct 24 – Nov 21**
- No matter what you're here to accomplish, this sun sign will flavor your path with intensity, sexuality, and charisma. Use those gifts to shed light on the unseen world and guide others through traumatic pain – which doesn't intimidate you. Your healing & insightful visions carry a depth of understanding that the world needs to embrace.

Sun Sign Meanings

- **Sagittarius (Archer) = Nov 22 - Dec 21**
- You can start up a conversation with anyone - from the president of the United Nations to a computer nerd. Yet don't let your social personality pull you from your mission and sidetrack you. Your social gifts are on purpose - to help you succeed as a teacher and visionary.
- **Capricorn (Goat) = Dec 22 – Jan 19**
- You came here to immerse yourself in the earthy, practical details of day-to-day reality. That gift of plodding determination, coupled with your intense focus on what you want, will get you where you want to go. Loosen your grip on mundane details and you will fulfill your potential.

Sun Sign Meanings

- **Aquarius (Water Bearer) = Jan 20 – Feb 18**
- Your ability to teach and inspire others with new ideas is paramount on this path. Use these great strengths to change the world. Take classes, read great books, surround yourself with thought-provoking people.

- **Pisces (Fish) = February 19 – March 20**
- Profound intuition and innate spiritual wisdom are your gifts – no matter what your mission is. Whenever you stifle that intuition to fit in, you're off path. Be sure to focus those intense feelings on the highest wisdom and don't get lost in your sensitivity.

Your Soul Agreements

- Your birth path: 7
- Your partner's birth path: 3
- 7 + 3 = 10
- Total: 10
- Reduced to a single digit: 1
- Your relationship number: 1
- Your relationship sum number explains your soul agreement with that person.

Your Soul Agreements

- If your relationship sum or soul agreement number is 1 it means:
- You'll both be empowered to own your truth and find your voice through this partnership. There will be enough space between you for each of you to grow and evolve independently. The challenge will be creating intimacy and truly connecting with one another. Instead, you may feel lonely and disconnected even though you're very happy in your own skin.
- If your soul agreement is 2 it means:
- Your challenge and your gift will be connecting deeply with each other. This will be the downfall or the salvation of your union. You're both very sensitive and intuitive and can be hurt easily. Once you move beyond the hurt to open your hearts to each other, you'll bond at such a deep level that you'll carry the other one in your heart every day.
- If your soul agreement is 11 it means:
- You'll have a powerful intuitive spiritual connection that you'll notice from day one. Together you'll create a healing business or platform to do your great work together. Your challenge will be the intense sensitivity that allows you to know each other's thoughts for better or worse. This requires honesty and shared positive thinking. If you're both spiritually evolved and focus your thoughts on love and gratitude, this could be a mystical union.

www.SueFrederick.com

Your Soul Agreements

- If your soul agreement is 3 it means:
- You'll have a great time together being social, creative, and brilliant. Your parties will be the most fun and your home will be luscious. Your friends will love you and you'll have trouble getting them to leave. Your brilliance will bounce off the walls and you'll enjoy many creative projects together. The problem will be moving from your heads (where you prefer to live) into your hearts and souls. Once you master this and learn to open your hearts to each other, to have feelings, you'll have a wonderful relationship.
- If your soul agreement is 4 it means:
- You can both be stubborn, strong, and willful. It will take a little work to open your hearts and connect. Sharing physical sports and outdoor adventures will bond you. You may decide to run a business together, and your daily dialog will likely be about your business rather than your feelings. This relationship will probably need weekly therapy or at least family meetings to keep all the parts in working order.
- If your soul agreement is 22 it means:
- You have huge work to share with the world through your partnership. You'll love being inspired together, taking classes, sharing books. You'll want friends who are spiritually inclined and open to new ideas. Together you have a responsibility to teach what you've learned through your powerful, shared career.

Your Soul Agreements

- If your soul agreement is 5 it means:

- You have a passionate, sensual connection and love sharing food, music, and travel. This could be a life of pleasure and passion if you're both spiritually strong and aren't tempted by addictions or infidelity. At your best, the two of you will lead a life of fun and travel. You may share a successful business in the natural health or adventure industries. At your worst, you'll lose your way with addictions, jealousy, and self-indulgences.

- If your soul agreement is 6 it means:

- There's possibility for deep, lasting love in this partnership. You'll have a warm, loving home and family that will be hugely important to both of you. But you each must remember who you are and spend some time apart. Otherwise, you risk losing your essential selves and forgetting your own missions and careers.

- If your soul agreement is 33 it means:

- You have a mystical connection--so mystical that you might not be able to make it work in everyday life. Being practical and getting bills paid will be the challenge. You share enormous artistic gifts and could create a project together that uplifts the world. Your shared true work will ultimately have a healing focus. Doing spiritual practices together is essential for your sanity and fulfillment.

Your Soul Agreements

- If your soul agreement is 7 it means:
- Your beautiful home will be refined, pristine, and elegant. You'll enjoy exploring spirituality and the arts together. You'll have a powerful intellectual connection and spend many hours analyzing life together. Don't let perfectionism destroy your love, though. You'll intuitively feel each other's energy and may sometimes be wounded by this powerful connection. Opening your hearts to share true warmth and intimacy will be the challenge.
- If your soul agreement is 8 it means:
- Power will be the game you play with each other--for better or worse. Your passion and sexuality will be so powerful it may take you out of the bounds of convention and into dangerous territory. Yet you'll support each other's work and create true abundance together. The question will be: Is it true love or is it passion and power?
- If your soul agreement is 9 it means:
- Surrender everything and let the divine energy within you direct this one. You can't control it and you can't walk away from it. The revelations you get from this partnership will be the highest lessons of your lifetime. You'll someday find yourselves holding council for others who want to know how you've made love last. Your answer will be: Surrender with love.

Your Soul Agreements

- Is My Perfect Partner on the Same Path As Me?
- If you're a 1 path and you fall in love with another 1 path, there are advantages and disadvantages. Here's an overview of how souls on the same paths get along:
- 1 Path and 1 Path = 2
- Each of you will need and can provide lots of space and independence for your partner. You'll be more comfortable living parallel lives as best friends on a shared journey. True intimacy and chemistry may be lacking, but there's potential for deep respect and understanding between you. You intuit each other's inner motivations, so you'll make a great team. Give each other enough independence, and this partnership could be a fulfilling and lasting one.
- 2 Path and 2 Path = 4
- You both crave intimacy, and you'll be intuitively connected from the day you meet. You'll have organized, clean homes and love working together. You'll probably want to spend all your time together. But your deep sensitivity means you'll both keep getting your feelings hurt and there will be lots of drama. You'll have to work every day to clear up miscommunications and nurture each other's sensitivity.

Your Soul Agreements

- 3 Path and 3 Path = 6
- There's plenty of fun and creativity in this relationship, and you'll eventually long to start a family. But who's going to make a living? At your best, you'll create a business to share and make it successful with your creative ideas. You may argue about who runs the business and who gets to stay home with the kids. At your worst, you'll both be stuck in your heads with little emotional warmth between you. Yet the potential is here to help each other open up and heal many old wounds from the past while you create a loving home and family.

- 4 Path and 4 Path = 8
- Lots of work gets done in this partnership, and you'll both love exercising, hiking, and keeping fit. Your combined hard work will create great financial success. But beware of burying yourselves in the day-to-day drudgery. You may end up spending little time together because of your shared work addiction-- unless you work together. Because you're both so strong, you need help opening your hearts to each other. One of you will have to initiate relaxation, vacations, and love dates. Money and success will thrive in your partnership as long as you both do the work required and neither of you tries to control the other.

Your Soul Agreements

- 5 Path and 5 Path = 1

- You share great sensuality and a passionate love of food, music, sex, and adventure. But you'll each be tempted to go your own way. Fidelity will be an issue, so please don't allow drugs or alcohol in the house, or addictions may destroy your great chemistry. If you immerse yourselves in spirituality and your independent careers, you can have a lasting love. Your challenge will be pulling yourselves away from indulgences and the temptations of others. Focusing on healthy living and a daily meditation practice will save you.

- 6 Path and 6 Path = 3

- Family and home will be your primary focus, but if you can both launch careers as healers or artists, this could work. Be careful not to lose yourselves in each other or in the kids. Personal growth and a strong spiritual practice will keep you and your family happy and healthy. Your shared creativity will spark plenty of brilliant new ideas such as artistic projects, home design and remodeling, and healthy gourmet cooking.

Your Soul Agreements

- 7 Path and 7 Path = 5
- Picture Einstein discussing quantum physics with Niels Bohr and you get the picture of what's possible here: two brilliant minds analyzing the world together. But unless one of you opens your heart, this relationship could be a cold one. You'll agree on lots of things, love the same hobbies, and want the same peaceful, elegant living space. But getting out of your heads will be the challenge. Once you learn to quiet your minds, enormous physical passion is possible. And if you each embrace spirituality and intuition, your passion will take on an otherworldly connection that will feed your soul.
- 8 Path and 8 Path = 7
- Unless you're highly evolved, this could be an abusive power struggle as you battle each other for control. If you're spiritually conscious beings and you've already owned your power in the world, this enlightened partnership can result in huge success and joint philanthropic endeavors. But you'll need lots of space between you to reduce the competitive friction. Respecting and empowering each other to do big work is essential for happiness. Exploring and practicing daily spiritual exercises, such as meditation or prayer, is required to make this partnership thrive and prosper.

Your Soul Agreements

- 9 Path and 9 Path = 9

- You're two wise old souls joining hands to save the world. You have deep simpatico and a shared wisdom from lifetimes of challenges and successes. Humanitarian work is essential for both of you. Launch a non-profit foundation together or become Science of the Mind ministers. It's essential that you both embrace your spirituality and step away from disappointments and past losses. If you can do this, the wisdom and love you share will be deeply fulfilling, but there will be lots of surrender required to make it work.

- 11 Path and 11 Path = 22/4

- The intensity of your sensitivities and the high frequency of your energy will generate great sparks and passion, but this relationship must help both of you use your gifts to change the world. If not, you may end up destroying each other with your high-voltage energy. If you're both spiritually evolved, you could create a partnership of twin souls reaching for the highest light in shared work and love.

Your Soul Agreements

- 22 Path and 22 Path = 8
- Let's change the world together and generate enormous abundance for everyone! That seems to be the agreement here. Imagine a household with two Oprahs or two Donald Trumps. Who's going to answer the phone? You will have so much important work to get done that you'll definitely need to hire a cook and housekeeper. Your brilliant ideas and inspiring conversations will flow endlessly through the day and into the night. Fascinating, high-powered friends will fill your dinner table. You won't have patience for trivia or fools. If you do your great work together, you will change the world and become one of the wealthiest couples in the world.
- 33 Path and 33 Path = 3
- This connection will at first feel energized and fun--but I caution against it. There's a distinct possibility of both of you becoming untethered from reality, a shift precipitated by drugs, alcohol, or spiritual practices. Your creativity and artistic gifts are enormous. Someone has to keep your feet on the ground. Who will feed you and pay the bills? You're the great explorers of the unknown realms, but you must also bring that knowledge back to Planet Earth in a healing way--and that takes work. If you're both deeply immersed in powerful spiritual work, this relationship could work. You can be shamans, saints, and artists who together heal the world.
- For more info about Soul Agreements please read my book I See Your Soul Mate

Your Name Number

- Every letter of the alphabet has a numerological vibration according to Pythagoras' method.
- When you add the numbers associated with the **vowels** in your name you get your **"soul's longing"** number.
- When you add the numbers associated with the **consonants** in your name you get your **"personality"** number.
- When you add the **total of both** the consonants and vowels in your name you get your **"essential vibration"** number.
- When you calculate the **missing numbers** from your name - you understand the **challenges** you've included in your birth plan.

Calculate Your Name Number

1	2	3	4	5	6	7	8	9
A	B	C	D	E	F	G	H	I
J	K	L	M	N	O	P	Q	R
S	T	U	V	W	X	Y	Z	

The name numbers can also be summarized like this:

1– A, J, S
2– B, K, T
3– C, L, U
4– D, M, V
5– E, N, W
6– F, O, X
7– G, P, Y
8– H, Q, Z
9– I, R

Calculate Your Name Number

1	2	3	4	5	6	7	8	9
A	B	C	D	E	F	G	H	I
J	K	L	M	N	O	P	Q	R
S	T	U	V	W	X	Y	Z	

JANE ANN CROSBY

Vowels = Soul's Longing number = 13/4
Consonants = Personality number = 11/2
Total of both = Essential Vibration – 15/6

Calculate Your Name Number

1	2	3	4	5	6	7	8	9
A	B	C	D	E	F	G	H	I
J	K	L	M	N	O	P	Q	R
S	T	U	V	W	X	Y	Z	

```
    1   5 1            1          6              = 13/4
   JANe         ANN         CROSBy     = 38/11/2
    1   5              55         39  127       = 6
```

Calculate Your Name Number

1	2	3	4	5	6	7	8	9
A	B	C	D	E	F	G	H	I
J	K	L	M	N	O	P	Q	R
S	T	U	V	W	X	Y	Z	

Calculate the **MISSING NUMBERS in your name**:

Jane Ann Crosby

1	2	3	4	5	6	7	8	9
4	1	1	0	4	1	1	0	1

She's missing 4s and 8s

She has the most 5s and 1s

Calculate Your Name Number

```
1 2 3 4 5 6 7 8 9
A B C D E F G H I
J K L M N O P Q R
S T U V W X Y Z
```

Calculate the **missing numbers in your name**:

Your Name:

1 2 3 4 5 6 7 8 9

How many 1s are in your name? Put that number beneath the 1 in the chart above. Continue with each number.

- What numbers are you missing?
- What numbers do you have the most of?

YOUR PINNACLE CYCLES

- During your life you experience **Four Pinnacle Cycles**.
- During each pinnacle cycle there will be one major lesson or goal that takes precedence in your life.
- This pinnacle number is pushing your soul to grow in a specific area at specific points in your life journey.

CALCULATE YOUR PINNACLE NUMBERS

- The following page explains how you calculate the Pinnacle Numbers or soul lessons you'll be focusing on during the four pinnacle stages of your life.

- This example uses birthdate **Sept 15, 1951**

CALCULATE YOUR PINNACLE NUMBERS

- **First Pinnacle number:**
  Month of Birth + date of birth:
  9 + 15 = 24 = **6**

- **Second Pinnacle number:**
  Day of Birth + year of birth:
  15 + 1951 = 1966 = **22/4**

- **Third Pinnacle number:**
  First Pinnacle number + Second Pinnacle number:
  6 + 4 = 10 = **1**

- **Fourth Pinnacle number:**
  Month of birth + year of birth:
  9 + 7 (1951) = 16 = **7**

CALCULATE YOUR PINNACLE CYCLES

	Your First Pinnacle runs from	Your Second Pinnacle runs from	Your Third Pinnacle runs from	Your Fourth Pinnacle runs from
Your Life Path is 1	age 0 - 35	age 35 - 44	age 44 - 53	age 53 -
Your Life Path is 2	age 0 - 34	age 34 - 43	age 43 - 52	age 52 -
Your Life Path is 3	age 0 - 33	age 33 - 42	age 42 - 51	age 51 -
Your Life Path is 4	age 0 - 32	age 32 - 41	age 41 - 50	age 50 -
Your Life Path is 5	age 0 - 31	age 31 - 40	age 40 - 49	age 49 -
Your Life Path is 6	age 0 - 30	age 30 - 39	age 39 - 48	age 48 -
Your Life Path is 7	age 0 - 29	age 29 - 38	age 38 - 47	age 47 -
Your Life Path is 8	age 0 - 28	age 28 - 37	age 37 - 46	age 46 -
Your Life Path is 9	age 0 - 27	age 27 - 36	age 36 - 45	age 45 -
Your Life Path is 11	age 0 - 34	age 34 - 43	age 43 - 52	age 52 -
Your Life Path is 22	age 0 - 32	age 32 - 41	age 41 - 50	age 50 -

6   22   1   7

www.SueFrederick.com

Personal Year Cycles

- Every year of your life you've been under the influence of a particular number - **1 through 9, 11, 22 or 33.**

- You're working with a different type of energy each year within a repeating nine-year cycle.

- These **nine-year cycles** are designed to move you through cycles of necessary reinvention; helping you master the challenges you signed up for and accomplish the work you came here to do.

Personal Year Calculation

- **Your current personal year** is determined by the single-digit numbers of your birth month and birth date added to the current calendar year and reduced to a single digit or master number.

  Example: **Birth date Sept 15, 1951**

- Month: Sept = 9
- Date: 15 = 6
- Current Year: 2023 = 7
- 9 + 6 + 7 = 22 = 22/4
- **Personal year 22/4**

Calculate Your Personal Year

- Your birth month:
- Your birth day:
- The current calendar year:
- Total:
- Reduced to a single digit:
- This is your personal year:

Meaning of Personal Years

- **Personal Year 1:**
- This is an important new beginning: launch your business, get a new job or title, start a graduate program, or move to a new location.
  Everything you do this year will influence the events of your life for the next nine years. There's lots of new energy helping you change directions. There's never been a better time for reinvention. This is also a year of intense self-focus, personal development, and cultivation of talents. Everything evolves around you and is dependent upon you. Have courage to make important decisions and move forward bravely – like a pioneer. At times you may feel alone, but this year demands that you work mostly alone.

- **Personal Year 2:**
- This is the year for cooperating with others to develop the vision you started last year. It's a slower, more gestative year – nurturing what you've already started rather than launching new things. Collect and assimilate data, and organize details. Your success hinges on working with and cooperating with others. Be receptive. Soften the forceful energy you thrived on last year. You might feel highly sensitive this year and develop warm friendships – even romances.

- **Personal Year 11:**
- In this highly charged year of personal illumination, your intellect is capable of achieving its greatest capacity – as well as intense psychic perception and artistic creation. Inspiration and revelation are yours to create with. The spiritual, psychic and artistic are your focus, and meditation or prayer will enhance all of your gifts. Refine your tastes, collect art, associate with creative people. This is not your best year for commercial success, but rather for inner evolution of your spiritual, intuitive, and artistic gifts.

Meaning of Personal Year

- **Personal Year 3:**
- This is a social, playful year, full of social events and new interests. Express yourself, get into the center of things, entertain groups. Forget long-term planning and just enjoy life; don't make important decisions about your future. The performing arts will call you, and it's time to look your best. Develop your skills with words – written or spoken. Life is your stage – enjoy it! Whatever you started in your one year is now reaping enjoyment for you. It's your year to blossom.

- **Personal Year 4:**
- It's time to get to work in this serious and responsible year. Get practical, establish organization and efficiency systems, build the foundation for future growth, set a budget, and do the physical work. Focus on the physical details of getting your home in order – whether that means moving, remodeling or cleaning. Engage in fitness and sports activities. Dependability and responsibility are your keys to success.

- **Personal Year 22:**
- This year your greatest aspirations and inspirations will be put into practical reality. You'll be bringing your most advanced ideas to a realistic and workable form. Humanity and society as a whole will benefit from your work, if you choose to step up to the plate. It's a year of putting personal concerns aside and doing your best for the world at large. Make big plans and introduce enormous changes. By focusing on the positive vibrations of this number, you'll have the opportunity to ascend to your greatest career achievements and acquire abundant financial rewards. You'll also feel the sting of criticism that greatness attracts. Focus on your work and keep moving forward.

Meaning of Personal Year

- **Personal Year 5:**
- Get ready for expansion, adventure, and the unexpected in this turning-point year. During this fast-moving, action- packed time, you'll be happiest and doing your best work when everything is changing around you. Take trips, investigate opportunities, and get rid of anything that is monotonous or boring. Eliminate conditions and people that are holding you back. Make room for the new. Focus on freedom and adapting to change. Enjoy this sensual year with many opportunities for physical indulgence. You'll be super-charged, attractive, and sexual. Revive your relationships or work circumstances with new energy.

- **Personal Year 6:**
- In this more responsible year, you'll take care of the important people in your life and career. Rather than focus on yourself, you'll adjust to the needs of others and enjoy group activities as you shift away from the sensual and passionate excesses of the 5 year. Marriage and close friendships will blossom due to your efforts to understand the people in your life. Let go of superficiality and take responsibility for yourself and others. Yet don't take on more than you can carry, or you'll fall into depression and overwhelm. This is one year, though, when general harmony is more important than your own needs.

- **Personal Year 7:**
- Enjoy this sabbatical from the physical aspects of life and focus your attention on the study of abstract ideas, science, mysticism, spirituality and artistic endeavors. Withdraw from the center of things and write books, go to school, meditate, and do research. Refine what you began in this nine-year-cycle by analyzing and perfecting projects, relationships, and goals. Your intuition will be at its most powerful – rely on it for all decisions. Pursue nothing; you will naturally attract what is meant to be in your life.

Meaning of Personal Year

- **Personal Year 8:**
- The serenity and reflection of the 7 year is over as you jump head-first into the world of career, power and money. If you wrote a book last year, this is the year to promote and sell it. If you researched and developed your new business last year, now is the time to get it funded. Physical accomplishment and material success are your focus, as you reap the seeds of success that you planted early in this nine- year-cycle. During this powerful year, claim recognition and take command to get concrete results. Think big, manage and direct others, move forward. Yet beware of abusing your power or becoming greedy. Be patient and generous to others - even if that feels tedious.

- **Personal Year 9:**
- This year you will wrap up what you started in your one-year. Lingering relationships will surface to be examined - then kept or discarded for the next cycle. Your career will conclude the focus that it's had for the past nine years, even though you won't see the new cycle just yet. Open your hands and let go, with faith that something new and better will arrive in your one year. You may be fired or laid off, or simply come to the end of a project you've worked on for years. Relationships will fall away or be transformed; and you'll grieve for your losses over the past nine years. Peace comes from higher wisdom and a greater connection to spirituality. The larger lessons of life will call to you, and your insights will be heightened. Use this awareness to benefit the people around you. Focus on artistic and spiritual disciplines, and wait for the new inspiration that begins soon in your approaching one-year.

- **Personal Year 33:**
- You'll be drawn to mystical knowledge, intuition, and spiritual guidance this year. But if you're not grounded, you could become disconnected to everyday reality. Stay away from alcohol and drugs, and meditate every day.

Saturn Returns

- At the **age of 27, 28, 29** you go through your **First Saturn Return**. This is a major transition point of the lifetime – your first true wake up moment of recognizing your journey for this lifetime and what it's really about – as opposed to what you thought it was about & the expectation of family & friends. It's your moment of seeing who you really are.

- At the **age of 57, 58, 59** you go through your **Second Saturn Return**. This is the second major transition point of your lifetime – where you are stripped naked until you are finally your true self in the world, not hiding behind any job titles or relationships – being the authentic self you came here to be - doing your great work in the world.

Reflection on Saturn Returns

- Ask yourself what was learned during the Saturn Return. It can open a deep understanding about the purpose of pain and how it fuels your life and great work.

- Saturn Returns are almost always a painful or intense time of transition that is long remembered – on purpose – to help us find our true path.

Self Review of Nine-Year Cycles

- One of the most helpful parts of numerology is reviewing your **previous nine-year cycles** and reflecting on what was occurring during each cycles.

- **Ask yourself:** How did this cycle begin & end? What was my intention at beginning of cycle? What did I let go of at end of cycle? What did I learn?

- What patterns do I see within my 9 year cycles?

1 Birth Path Chart

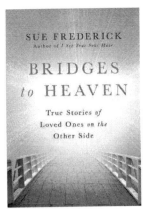

PY	AGE		PY	AGE		PY	AGE
1	0 years		1	27		1	54
2	1 year old		2	28 SR		2	55
3	2		3	29		3	56
4	3		4	30		4	57
5	4		5	31		5	58 SR
6	5		6	32		6	59
7	6		7	33		7	60
8	7		8	34		8	61
9	**8 years old**		**9**	**35**		**9**	**62**
1	9		1	36		1	63
2	10		2	37		2	64
3	11		3	38		3	65
4	12		4	39		4	66
5	13		5	40		5	67
6	14		6	41		6	68
7	15		7	42		7	69
8	16		8	43		8	70
9	**17**		**9**	**44**		**9**	**71**
1	18		1	45		1	72
2	19		2	46		2	73
3	20		3	47		3	74
4	21		4	48		4	75
5	22		5	49		5	76
6	23		6	50		6	77
7	24		7	51		7	78
8	25		8	52		8	79
9	26		9	53		9	80

www.SueFrederick.com

11 or 2 Birth Path Chart

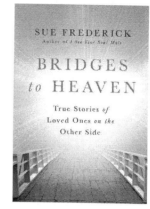

PY	AGE
2	0 years
3	1 year old
4	2
5	3
6	4
7	5
8	6
9	**7**
1	8 years old
2	9
3	10
4	11
5	12
6	13
7	14
8	15
9	**16**
1	17
2	18
3	19
4	20
5	21
6	22
7	23
8	24
9	**25**
1	26
2	27
3	28
4	29 SR
5	30
6	31
7	32
8	33
9	**34**
1	35
2	36
3	37
4	38
5	39
6	40
7	41
8	42
9	**43**
1	44
2	45
3	46
4	47
5	48
6	49
7	50
8	51
9	**52**
1	53
2	54
3	55
4	56
5	57
6	58 SR
7	59
8	60
9	**61**
1	62
2	63
3	64
4	65
5	66
6	67
7	68
8	69
9	**70**
1	71
2	72
3	73
4	74
5	75
6	76
7	77
8	78
9	**79**
1	80

3 Birth Path Chart

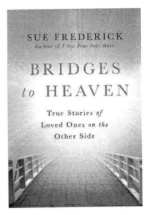

PY	AGE
3	0 years
4	1 year old
5	2
6	3
7	4
8	5
9	**6**
1	7
2	8 years old
3	9
4	10
5	11
6	12
7	13
8	14
9	**15**
1	16
2	17
3	18
4	19
5	20
6	21
7	22
8	23
9	**24**
1	25
2	26
3	27
4	28
5	29 SR
6	30
7	31
8	32
9	**33**
1	34
2	35
3	36
4	37
5	38
6	39
7	40
8	41
9	**42**
1	43
2	44
3	45
4	46
5	47
6	48
7	49
8	50
9	**51**
1	52
2	53
3	54
4	55
5	56
6	57
7	58
8	59 SR
9	**60**
1	61
2	62
3	63
4	64
5	65
6	66
7	67
8	68
9	**69**
1	70
2	71
3	72
4	73
5	74
6	75
7	76
8	77
9	**78**
1	79
2	80

www.SueFrederick.com

22 or 4 Birth Path Chart

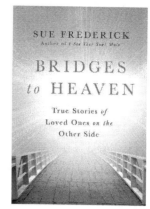

PY	AGE
4	0 years
5	1 year old
6	2
7	3
8	4
9	**5**
1	6
2	7
3	8 years old
4	9
5	10
6	11
7	12
8	13
9	**14**
1	15
2	16
2	17
4	18
4	19
5	20
7	21
8	22
9	**23**
1	24
2	25
3	26
4	27
5	28
6	29 SR
7	30
8	31
9	**32**
1	33
2	34
3	35
4	36
5	37
6	38
7	39
8	40
9	**41**
1	42
2	43
3	44
4	45
5	46
6	47
7	48
8	49
9	**50**
1	51
2	52
3	53
4	54
5	55
6	56
7	57
8	58
9	**59 SR**
1	60
2	61
3	62
4	63
5	64
6	65
7	66
8	67
9	**68**
1	69
2	70
3	71
4	72
5	73
6	74
7	75
8	76
9	**77**
1	78
2	79
3	80

5 Birth Path Chart

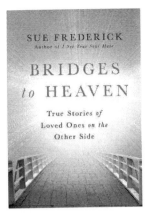

PY	AGE
5	0 years
6	1 year old
7	2
8	3
9	**4**
1	5
2	6
3	7
4	8 years old
5	9
6	10
7	11
8	12
9	**13**
1	14
2	15
3	16
4	17
5	18
6	19
7	20
8	21
9	**22**
1	23
2	24
3	25
4	26
5	27
6	28
7	29 SR
8	30
9	**31**
1	32
2	33
3	34
4	35
5	36
6	37
7	38
8	39
9	**40**
1	41
2	42
3	43
4	44
5	45
6	46
7	47
8	48
9	**49**
1	50
2	51
3	52
4	53
5	54
6	55
7	56
8	57
9	**58 SR**
1	59
2	60
3	61
4	62
5	63
6	64
7	65
8	66
9	**67**
1	68
2	69
3	70
4	71
5	72
6	73
7	74
8	75
9	**76**
1	77
2	78
3	79
4	80

www.SueFrederick.com

33 or 6 Birth Path Chart

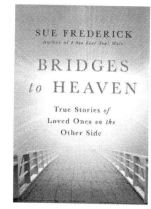

PY	AGE		PY	AGE		PY	AGE
6	0 years		6	27		6	54
7	1 year old		7	28		7	55
8	2		8	29 SR		8	56
9	**3**		**9**	**30**		**9**	**57 SR**
1	4		1	31		1	58
2	5		2	32		2	59
3	6		3	33		3	60
4	7		4	34		4	61
5	8 years old		5	35		5	62
6	9		6	36		6	63
7	10		7	37		7	64
8	11		8	38		8	65
9	**12**		**9**	**39**		**9**	**66**
1	13		1	40		1	67
2	14		2	41		2	68
3	15		3	42		3	69
4	16		4	43		4	70
5	17		5	44		5	71
6	18		6	45		6	72
7	19		7	46		7	73
8	20		8	47		8	74
9	**21**		**9**	**48**		**9**	**75**
1	22		1	49		1	76
2	23		2	50		2	77
3	24		3	51		3	78
4	25		4	52		4	79
5	26		5	53		5	80

www.SueFrederick.com

7 Birth Path Chart

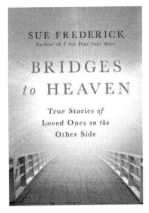

PY	AGE
7	0 years
8	1 year old
9	2
1	3
2	4
3	5
4	6
5	7
6	8 years old
7	9
8	10
9	11
1	12
2	13
3	14
4	15
5	16
6	17
7	18
8	19
9	20
1	21
2	22
3	23
4	24
5	25
6	26
7	27
8	28
9	29 SR
1	30
2	31
3	32
4	33
5	34
6	35
7	36
8	37
9	38
1	39
2	40
3	41
4	42
5	43
6	44
7	45
8	46
9	47
1	48
2	49
3	50
4	51
5	52
6	53
7	54
8	55
9	56
1	57 SR
2	58
3	59
4	60
5	61
6	62
7	63
8	64
9	65
1	66
2	67
3	68
4	69
5	70
6	71
7	72
8	73
9	74
1	75
2	76
3	77
4	78
5	79
6	80

www.SueFrederick.com

8 Birth Path Chart

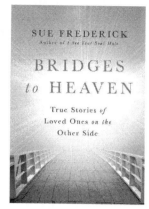

PY	AGE
8	0 years
9	1 year old
1	2
2	3
3	4
4	5
5	6
6	7
7	8 years old
8	9
9	10
1	11
2	12
3	13
4	14
5	15
6	16
7	17
8	18
9	19
1	20
2	21
3	22
4	23
5	24
6	25
7	26
8	27
9	28 SR
1	29
2	30
3	31
4	32
5	33
6	34
7	35
8	36
9	37
1	38
2	39
3	40
4	41
5	42
6	43
7	44
8	45
9	46
1	47
2	48
3	49
4	50
5	51
6	52
7	53
8	54
9	55
1	56
2	57
3	58 SR
4	59
5	60
6	61
7	62
8	63
9	64
1	65
2	66
3	67
4	68
5	69
6	70
7	71
8	72
9	73
1	74
2	75
3	76
4	77
5	78
6	79
7	80

www.SueFrederick.com

9 Birth Path Chart

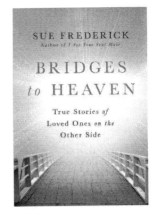

PY	AGE		PY	AGE		PY	AGE
9	0 years		9	27 SR		9	54
1	1 year old		1	28		1	55
2	2		2	29		2	56
3	3		3	30		3	57
4	4		4	31		4	58 SR
5	5		5	32		5	59
6	6		6	33		6	60
7	7		7	34		7	61
8	8 years old		8	35		8	62
9	9		9	36		9	63
1	10		1	37		1	64
2	11		2	38		2	65
3	12		3	39		3	66
4	13		4	40		4	67
5	14		5	41		5	68
6	15		6	42		6	69
7	16		7	43		7	70
8	17		8	44		8	71
9	18		9	45		9	72
1	19		1	46		1	73
2	20		2	47		2	74
3	21		3	48		3	75
4	22		4	49		4	76
5	23		5	50		5	77
6	24		6	51		6	78
7	25		7	52		7	79
8	26		8	53		8	80

Made in the USA
Middletown, DE
19 February 2024

50030486R00046